A Tree Can Be...

Written by Judy Nayer
Pictures by Anna Vojtech

SCHOLASTIC INC.

New York   Toronto   London   Auckland   Sydney

Copyright © 1994 by Scholastic Inc.
All rights reserved. Published by Scholastic Inc.
Printed in the U.S.A.
ISBN 0-590-27377-9

2 3 4 5 6 7 8 9 10   09   00 99 98 97 96 95 94

A tree can be . . .

a place to play,

4

a place to rest,

5

a place to hide,

and a place to nest.

A tree can be . . .
a place to swing,

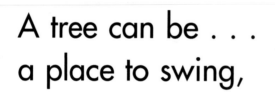

a place to fly,

a place to climb,

and a place to stay dry.

A tree can be . . .
a place full of food,

a place full of sound,

a place full of life,

and it changes year-round.

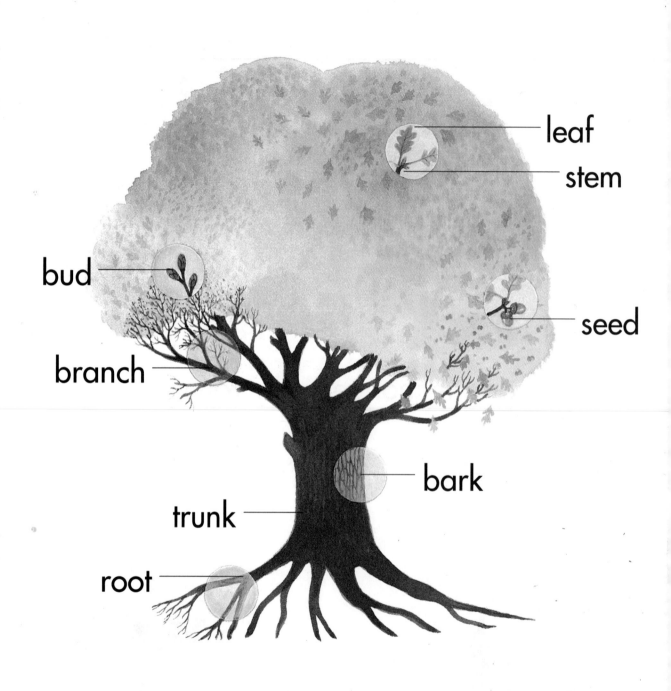

leaf

stem

bud

seed

branch

bark

trunk

root

An oak tree